CRABS

by Herbert S. Zim
and Lucretia Krantz

ILLUSTRATIONS BY RENÉ MARTIN

William Morrow and Company

New York 1974

For their help in supplying data and checking the manuscript, the authors wish to thank Dr. Waldo Schmidt and Dr. A. F. Chase of the U.S. National Museum, Smithsonian Institute, and Dr. George E. Krantz, University of Miami.

Printed in the United States of America.
1   2   3   4   5   78   77   76   75   74

Library of Congress Cataloging in Publication Data

Zim, Herbert Spencer (date)
   Crabs.

   SUMMARY: Describes the characteristics of the many species of crabs and briefly discusses their commercial importance.
   1. Crabs — Juvenile literature. [1. Crabs] I. Krantz, Lucretia, joint author. II. Martin, René, fl. 1965-   illus.   II. Title.
QL444.M33Z55   595'.3842   73-16328
ISBN 0-688-20114-8
ISBN 0-688-30114-2 (lib. bdg.)

AMPHIBIOUS CRAB

Everyone visiting the seashore has seen crabs. Those on the sand or in the water are only a few of the hundreds of kinds that are found in nearly all parts of the world.

Crabs live in the arctic and the tropics, on land, in trees, in shallow water, and in the complete darkness of the deepest ocean. Some live in burrows and even inside other sea animals. Several kinds of crabs share their homes with other creatures. Still others carry shell houses on their backs.

female

male

FIDDLER CRAB

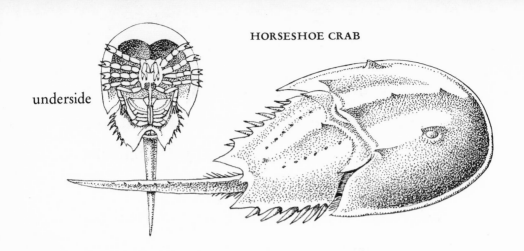

underside

You can look and find big crabs and little crabs, fast crabs and slow crabs, crabs that walk and crabs that swim. Some so-called crabs, like the horseshoe crab, are not crabs at all. The largest is the crab in the sky, the constellation called Cancer. This immense imaginary crab can be seen toward the south on spring nights.

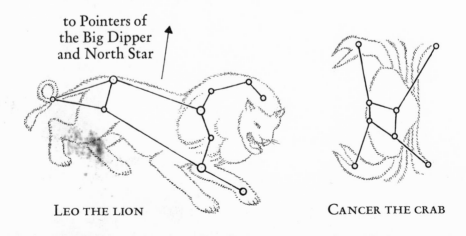

to Pointers of
the Big Dipper
and North Star

LEO THE LION

CANCER THE CRAB

Despite the fact that crabs are widespread and common, they form only one small part of the world's largest animal group — arthropods, or joint-legged animals. About 85 percent of all animals, well over a million kinds, belong in this group. It includes a vast host of insects, spiders, scorpions, centipedes, and the famous extinct trilobites. These extinct arthropods were as common as crabs 600 million years ago. Still, another 350 million years passed before the first true crabs appeared.

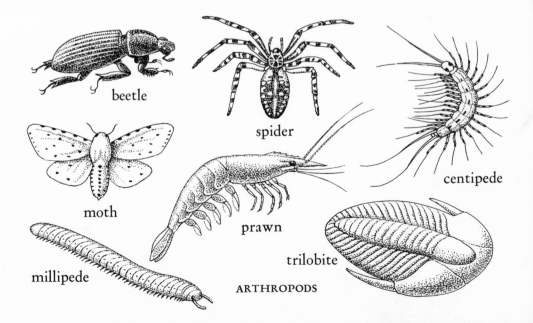

beetle

spider

centipede

moth

prawn

trilobite

millipede

ARTHROPODS

All crabs were once aquatic, living in the seas. Since the environment of the seas has remained much the same, crabs adapted to it have changed little. Those that moved to land show more changes, but females still return to the seas to spawn or lay eggs.

Scientists think of arthropods as composed of five large groups, each different although with many things in common. One is the crustaceans, a group of some 25,000 kinds or species, including the crabs. Crustaceans have segmented bodies with their skeletons outside, and jointed legs. The skeletons are composed of chitin, a tough, hard, or horny material. To grow, all crustaceans shed their old skeleton and form a new, larger one. They breathe through gills. Their bodies have two major parts.

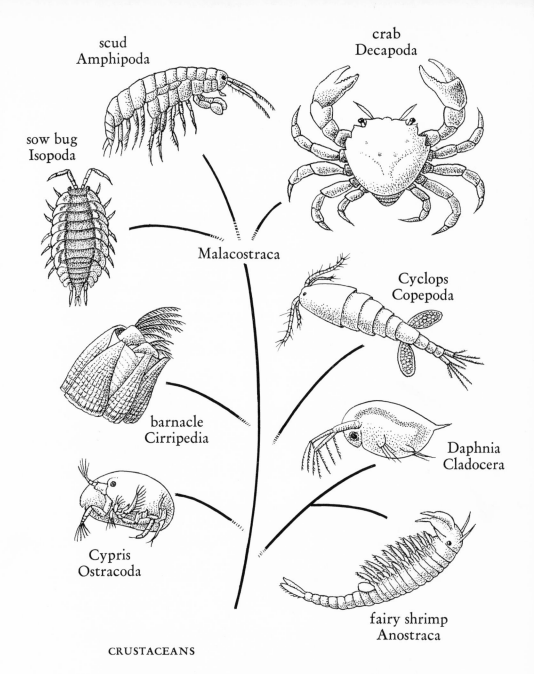

scud
Amphipoda

crab
Decapoda

sow bug
Isopoda

Malacostraca

Cyclops
Copepoda

barnacle
Cirripedia

Daphnia
Cladocera

Cypris
Ostracoda

fairy shrimp
Anostraca

CRUSTACEANS

Some 26,000 kinds of crustaceans are classified
into about 30 groups or orders. One of these,
the decapods, includes crabs, shrimps, and lobsters.

Your body has two divisions also, a head and a trunk, to which your four limbs are attached. An insect has three body divisions, a head, an abdomen, and a thorax to which six legs are attached. Crustaceans have their head and thorax fused together, but the abdomen remains separate.

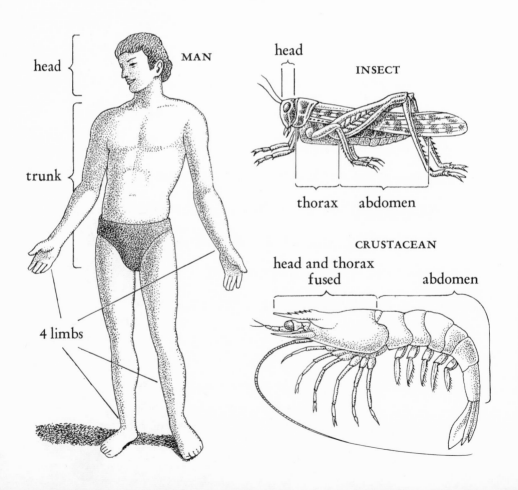

head

MAN

trunk

4 limbs

head

INSECT

thorax   abdomen

CRUSTACEAN

head and thorax
fused   abdomen

Crabs and other crustaceans come from wormlike ancestors with bodies that have rings, or segments. These segments can still be seen among living crustaceans. The number of body segments varies, but there may be 20 or so. Each segment usually carries a pair of jointed legs. Some are walking legs or swimming paddles; others have become feelers and even mouthparts. The chewing parts of the mouth of crabs are formed from three pairs of modified legs.

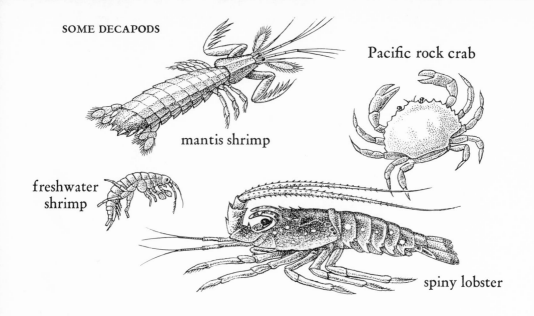

SOME DECAPODS

mantis shrimp

Pacific rock crab

freshwater shrimp

spiny lobster

Crabs and their close relatives are placed in one group of crustaceans, the Malacostraca. Within this large group is a smaller one in which each animal has ten legs, used for walking, grasping, or swimming. These decapods, as they are called, because of their five pairs of legs, include crabs, shrimp, crayfish, lobsters, and their kin.

Crabs, however, are different from their decapod relatives in several ways. Some crabs live on land. No shrimps or lobsters do. The bodies of shrimps and lobsters are flatter, with longer, narrower, segmented abdomens. Crabs have short, broad, flattened bodies and different types of abdomens.

The most common kind of crab abdomen is short and hard. It is folded tightly under the body, as among the blue, spider, or calico crabs. The second kind, like that of the porcelain, mole, and coconut crabs, is large, hard, and tucks under the body. The third kind, that of the hermit crabs, is long and soft. It fits into the spiral chamber of sea-shells.

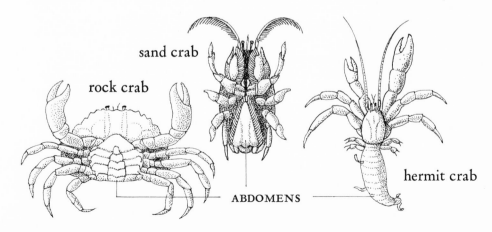

sand crab

rock crab

hermit crab

ABDOMENS

Male and female crabs look very much alike, but they can be told apart if you look carefully. The differences are in the shape of the shell, in some body structures, and in the color. The abdomen of the male crab is usually a narrow triangle, while that of the female is larger, oval or round, and protects her eggs.

Among the green crabs, some hermit crabs, and others, the male is larger than the female, and so each sex can be recognized. The male blue crab has blue-and-white tips to its claws, while the female has red. Male fiddler crabs have one small and one large

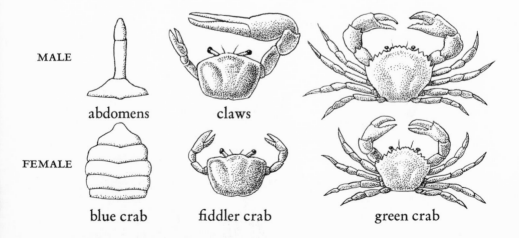

MALE   FEMALE

abdomens   claws

blue crab   fiddler crab   green crab

claw; the female's claws are both small. These differences may pass unnoticed unless one knows what to observe.

Besides differences in appearance, male and female crabs also show differences in behavior. They are best seen during courtship, when the male crab seeks a mate. The male fiddler crab waves his large claw in the air. Sometimes he raps the ground with it to attract a female. The male blue crab dances in front of the female with his claws outstretched. The male hermit crab grabs the female with his large claws and drags her around with him.

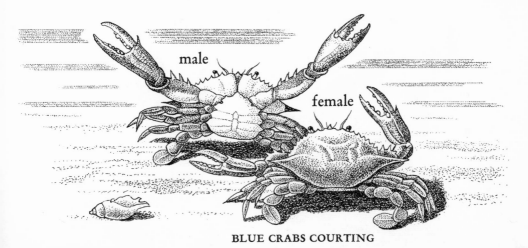

BLUE CRABS COURTING

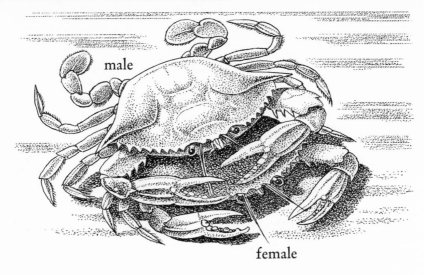

male

female

Courting behavior soon leads to mating, often while the female is in a soft-shell stage. The female receives sperm directly from the male, but she is able to store it in little "pockets" till egg-laying time, which may be weeks, months, or as much as a year later. When the female lays her eggs, she already has the sperm to fertilize them. The female blue crab mates only once, but receives enough sperm to fertilize millions of eggs. Crabs that live longer may mate each year.

A female blue crab may lay up to two million eggs at a time. The eggs pile up in a spongy mass under her oval abdomen, held in place by a kind of glue that forms while the eggs are laid. As more and more eggs are fertilized and pushed out, the abdomen is forced outward from the female's body. At this stage she is called a sponge crab. Most female crabs produce one set of eggs each summer, but blue crabs often lay two.

Eggs must be kept moist until they hatch. The female ghost crab has a problem, because she lives on the dry beach. After she deposits her eggs under her abdomen, she must keep running into the water to wet them.

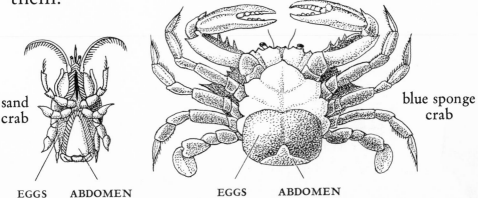

sand
crab

blue sponge
crab

EGGS   ABDOMEN   EGGS   ABDOMEN

Other land crabs return to the water to lay their eggs and remain there till the eggs hatch in about two weeks. Then the tiny free-swimming young larvae escape and live in the water, feeding and passing through several stages of growth. A few species of freshwater crabs do not have free-swimming larvae. Their young emerge from the eggs as miniature adults and just increase in size as they grow.

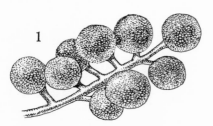

orange eggs
eleven days before hatching

dark-brown eggs
shortly before hatching

empty eggshells
after hatching

prezoea larva
after hatching

SOME EARLY STAGES AND LARVAL GROWTH OF BLUE CRABS
all greatly enlarged

In this first larval stage most crabs look very different from adults. The transparent larvae are about 1 millimeter long and float at the surface. They feed on plankton — very small marine plants and animals. During this stage, which lasts a month or more, a young crab larva may shed its tiny shell several times. Each time it grows a bit. As the mouthparts take on adult form, the crab passes into the second larval stage.

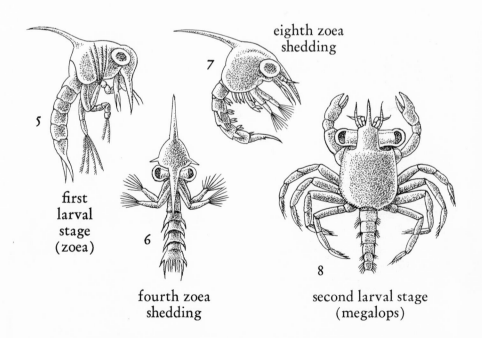

5 first larval stage (zoea)

6 fourth zoea shedding

7 eighth zoea shedding

8 second larval stage (megalops)

FIRST CRAB STAGE

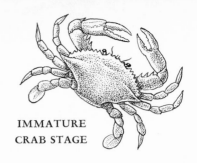

IMMATURE
CRAB STAGE

During the two months or so spent in the second stage, the young crab goes down to the bottom to live. When its shell is shed again, the young crab closely resembles an adult. It is soon feeding like one, and in a year or so will become an adult in every respect. A blue crab molts, or sheds its shell, about fifteen times in its larval stages. The fiddler crab sheds only twice, and other crabs have different growth patterns.

Molting enables crabs to grow, despite

MOLTING

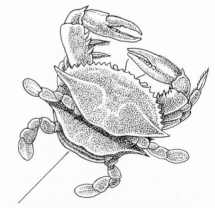

old shell beginning to split   crab starting to push itself out

their hard outer skeletons. To keep growing, a crab must cast off its rigid shell and replace it with a newer, larger one. But molting does not stop when the crabs are mature. Crabs continue to molt for their entire life.

As molting starts, a new soft shell grows inside the hard one. The old shell becomes loosened and begins to split in the back, leaving a gap between it and the abdomen. The shell continues to split on either side, and the crab, with its new soft shell, starts to push itself out. In a few minutes (but sometimes much longer) the crab is free. The old split shell is shed and left behind.

old shell

crab freeing itself from old shell

The new chitin shell is thin, soft, wrinkled, and elastic. While it is soft, the crab can grow. It gets larger by taking in an enormous amount of water. This increase in body fluids stretches the new shell to its full size and smooths out the wrinkles. Now the crab is bigger than before it molted. Slowly the fluids are replaced as the crab's tissues grow.

Molting crabs usually seek a spot safe from harm or attack till their thin shell hardens. This may take only a few hours or, among slow-growing crabs, as long as several days. Crabs are helpless with a soft shell. Their enemies, often other crabs, search for them on the grassy bottoms in shallow water.

discarded shell

soft and wrinkled crab

engorged with water

The crab shell, like that of all crustaceans, is made mostly of chitin. Chitin may be soft, thin, and even transparent as it forms. Later it becomes tough and leathery till it is something like the horn of cattle or even like your own fingernails. Most crab shells become as hard as rock due to chemical changes brought about by calcium in seawater. Once the new shell is hardened, the crab resumes its normal active life.

The number of times a crab molts and the time between molts differs with the crab's species and age. Crabs molt more often when they are young, have plenty of food, and when the water is warm. Larger, older crabs grow slowly and so molt less often.

hiding till shell hardens

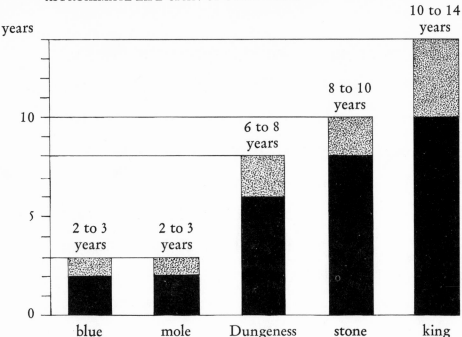

Little is known about the age of crabs, but ten years or so seems to be as long as any live. Blue crabs are known to live for three years, mole crabs for two years, and the small pea crabs for two to three years. Dungeness crabs, caught and sold along the Pacific coast, are reported to live for eight years.

Crabs show another interesting kind of growth that is called regeneration. They often lose one or more legs or claws, through accident or injury. If a leg or claw is injured, the crab can make it drop off at a definite place, called a breaking plane. The wound closes quickly, and little blood escapes.

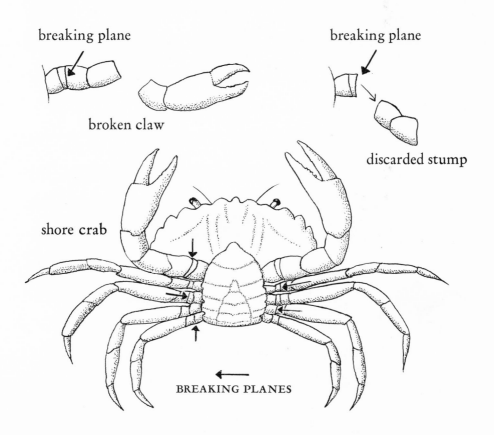

breaking plane

broken claw

breaking plane

discarded stump

shore crab

BREAKING PLANES

Regeneration of a new limb usually takes place at the breaking plane. The stump, if any, is lost during the next molt. After molting, the crab has a new, usable, but much smaller leg. Two or more molts are needed to form a leg or a claw of normal size. When a crab no longer molts, due to old age, it cannot regenerate a lost limb. People who fish for stone crabs often break off one claw to eat and throw the crab back so it can grow a new claw.

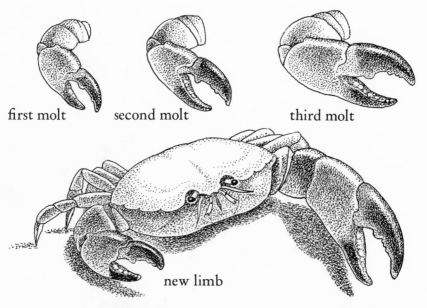

first molt   second molt   third molt

new limb

REGENERATION OF STONE-CRAB CLAW

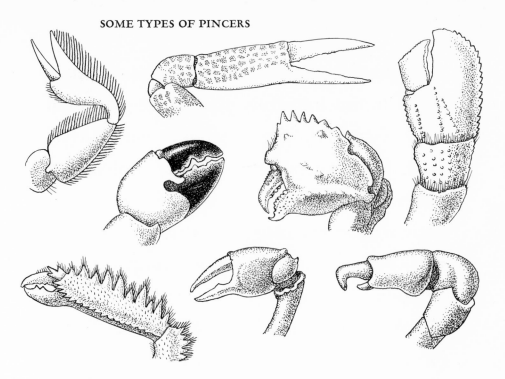

Crabs use their legs for getting around, but their claws, or pincers, which are the modified first pair of legs, have special uses in feeding and in courtship. Pincers are fine weapons too, as anyone who has been nipped by a crab knows. They are also used for climbing, for clinging to seaweed, and for moving small objects.

Crabs may walk or run on all ten of their legs — or on only two pairs of them. Many walk sidewise. The motion is hard to observe, but the leading legs are bent to *pull* while the trailing legs are stretched out to *push.* Crabs tend to have hairs or bristles on the ends of their legs. These help them to walk or climb over rocks or soft mud without slipping. Fiddler crabs move around in mud with ease.

GHOST CRAB RUNNING

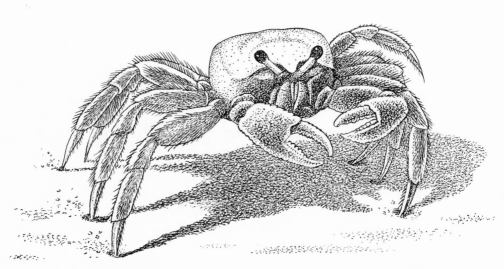

right legs pushing
left legs pulling

The fastest-running crabs are the ghost crabs, which live on dry shores and sand dunes. They can move at a speed of 1.6 meters a second, running on two or three pairs of legs. When running, they often turn their bodies halfway around to transfer the work load to the new leading legs. This turn is made without a pause, and then the legs that bend and pull begin to stretch and push instead.

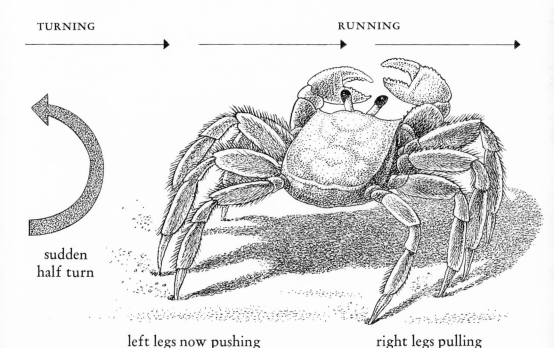

TURNING   RUNNING

sudden
half turn

left legs now pushing   right legs pulling

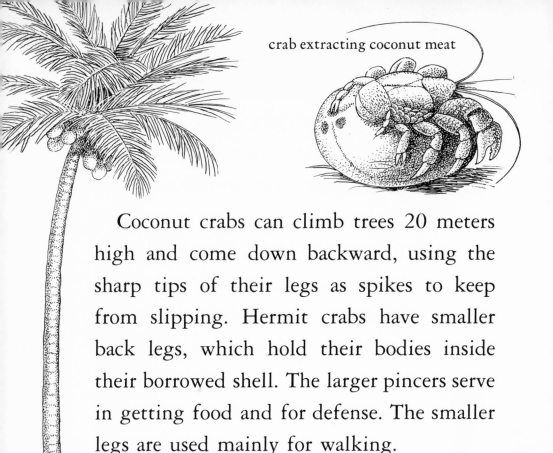

crab extracting coconut meat

Coconut crabs can climb trees 20 meters high and come down backward, using the sharp tips of their legs as spikes to keep from slipping. Hermit crabs have smaller back legs, which hold their bodies inside their borrowed shell. The larger pincers serve in getting food and for defense. The smaller legs are used mainly for walking.

COCONUT CRAB

Many crabs swim, and in the portunid family of swimming crabs the blue crab is the most powerful and agile. The speckled crab and the ornate crab are like it. The fifth pair of legs of these swimming crabs end in broad, flat paddles. The paddles are held out to the side and slightly above the shell. They are moved in a figure-eight pattern as the crab swims. The fourth pair of legs have no paddles, but they move in the same way and may help keep the crab from turning over or around as it swims.

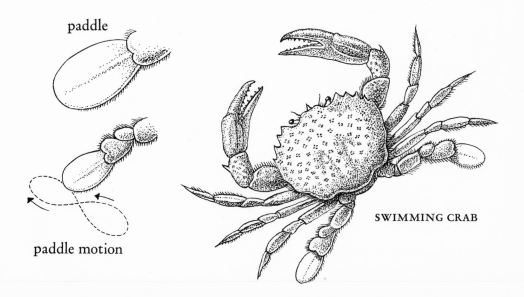

paddle

paddle motion

SWIMMING CRAB

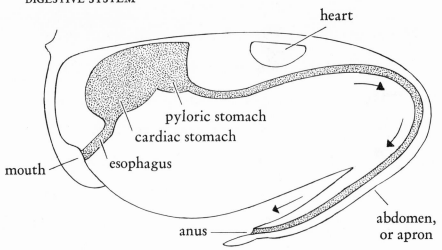

Crabs catch their food with their pincers. These pass the food to the mouth, which has three pairs of hard jaws. The first pair helps to hold the food while the other pairs cut and tear it into smaller pieces. The food then passes into the crab's double stomach, where a grinding action, aided by digestive juices, breaks the food down so that it can be digested. Undigested food passes through the intestines and out through the anus.

Some swimming crabs catch and eat fish, but most crabs hunt other small sea animals as food. Typical foods are those smaller creatures that live on the bottom. The mud crab and stone crab prey on small oysters and barnacles. Crabs also eat plants; some are wholly vegetarian. Other crabs are scavengers, feeding on any dead material they find. The coconut crab is one. It will eat the meat of coconuts that have been broken open or pierce the "eyes" through the hard shell and scoop out the inner layer with its legs.

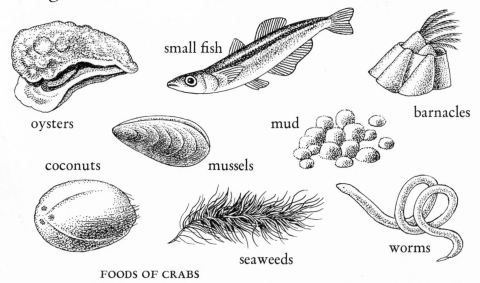

oysters

small fish

barnacles

coconuts

mussels

mud

seaweeds

worms

FOODS OF CRABS

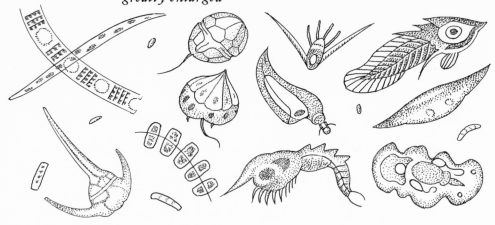

The pea and fiddler crabs are filter feeders. The pea crab lives inside the shells of oysters and clams. It uses its mouthparts to filter water currents inside the clamshell and obtain bits of food. The fiddler crab scoops up mud and debris with its pincers or its legs. This mixture goes into its mouth where it is sifted, filtered, and swallowed. The organic material is kept as food, and the mud is spit out as a round pellet. The mole crab filters tiny plants and debris from the surf water as waves wash over it on the beach.

Crabs breathe by means of gills. The number of gills varies with the species. Blue crabs have eight gills on each side of their bodies; pea crabs have only three. Crabs, like fish, take the oxygen from air that is dissolved in seawater. This oxygen is extracted as the water passes over blood vessels in the crab's gills. A current of water is produced by gill bailers, small paddles on the second pair of jaws. Crabs also have a brush of hairs on the other pair of jaws, to remove dirt from the gills. The water current can be reversed for cleaning the gills too.

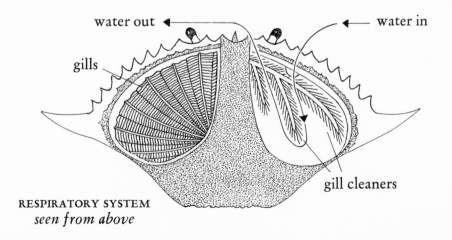

water out ◄—   ◄— water in

gills

gill cleaners

RESPIRATORY SYSTEM
seen from above

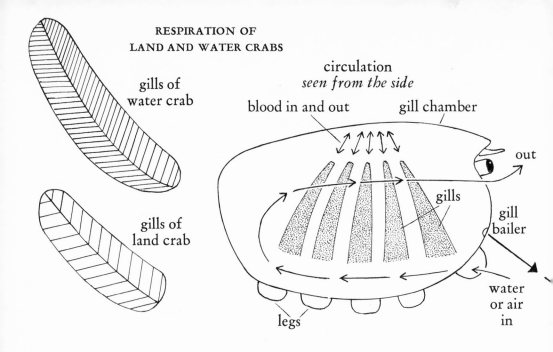

RESPIRATION OF
LAND AND WATER CRABS

gills of
water crab

circulation
seen from the side

blood in and out

gill chamber

out

gills

gills of
land crab

gill
bailer

water
or air
in

legs

Land crabs have smaller gills but larger blood vessels to absorb oxygen. The same type of gill bailers create a current of air over the gills instead of a current of water. Crabs that move back and forth from water to land fill their gill chambers with water. While they are on land, a current of air set up by the gill bailers adds oxygen to the water that they carry in their gills.

The crab's blood flows in and out of the gills, taking in oxygen and releasing carbon dioxide gas. Crabs have blue blood. The color is caused by a copper chemical that carries the oxygen. In human blood an iron chemical does the same work, but it gives our blood a red color.

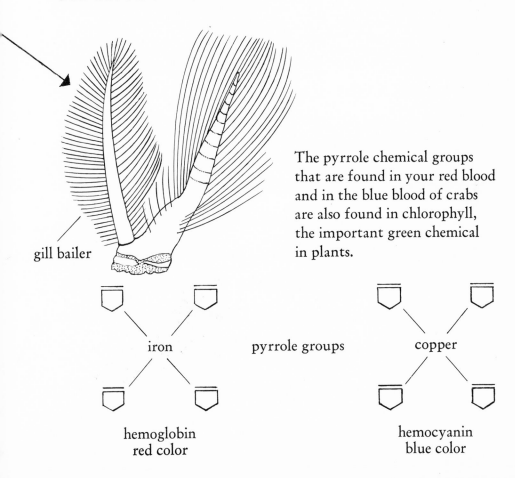

gill bailer

The pyrrole chemical groups that are found in your red blood and in the blue blood of crabs are also found in chlorophyll, the important green chemical in plants.

iron

pyrrole groups

copper

hemoglobin
red color

hemocyanin
blue color

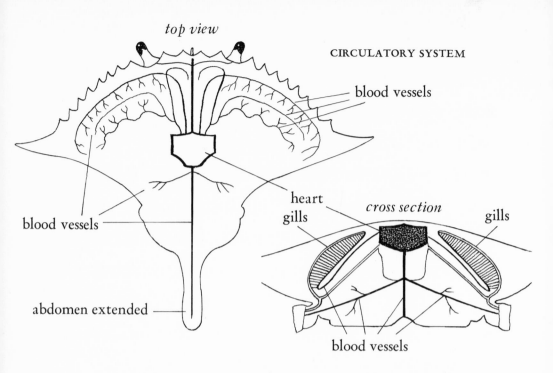

top view

blood vessels

blood vessels

heart

gills

cross section

gills

blood vessels

abdomen extended

The crab's blood moves from the gills to the heart. This simple heart in the middle of the crab's body is coffin-shaped and has only a single chamber. (The human heart has four chambers.) From the heart, the blood goes around the body and back to the gills again. This process may take about 40 to 60 seconds in a large crab.

Some crabs can make sounds, but none have a true sense of hearing. However, they seem to be able to detect vibrations in the air or water. Sounds are made by rubbing one part of the body against another or tapping legs on the ground. Ghost crabs make a creaking or filing sound by rubbing their claws together. It seems to be a warning sound similar to the one that fiddler crabs make.

The limited sounds that crabs make seem to warn others away from their territory, or they may attract females for mating.

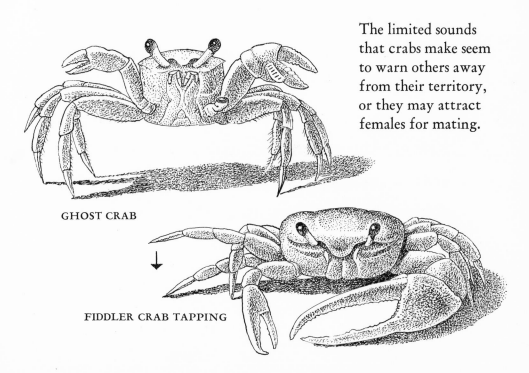

GHOST CRAB

FIDDLER CRAB TAPPING

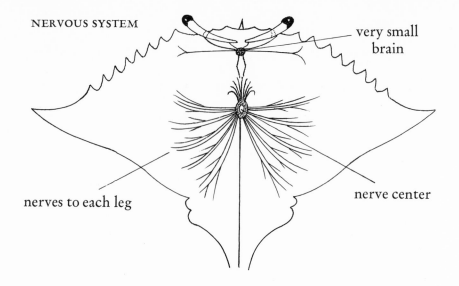

NERVOUS SYSTEM

very small
brain

nerves to each leg

nerve center

Crabs have a brain, but it is small and quite limited. Connected to it are nerves that go to sense organs and to all parts of the crab's body. Important to crabs are their eyes and balancing organs. The eyes are often on stalks. They can turn and can be pulled down into the eye sockets. Crabs do not see clearly the way we do. The balance organs are at the base of the antennae near the mouth.

The eyestalks of crabs also make messenger chemicals, or hormones. These, and the nerve cells of the crab, signal changes in the color of the crab's shell as seen among the fiddler, blue crab, and others. Crabs can change their color somewhat to blend better with the background. Red and yellow colors seem to be under the control of hormones, black and white under the control of nerves.

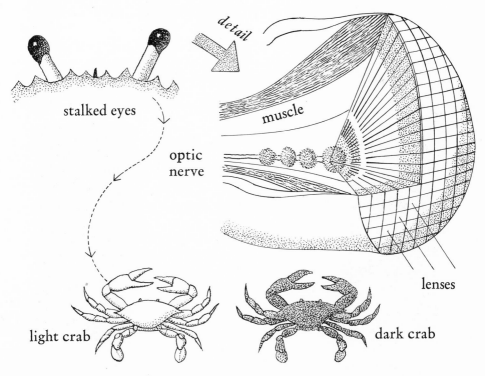

detail

stalked eyes

muscle

optic nerve

lenses

light crab

dark crab

COLOR INFLUENCED BY HORMONES FROM EYE STALKS

Crabs often change their color or their daily activities in a regular pattern that still baffles scientists. These changes are controlled by something called a "biological clock" within the crab. But what the clock is and how it works is a mystery. Fiddler crabs, for example, are dark during the day and much paler at night. But even if the crabs are kept in complete darkness, they change color regularly. Hormones controlled by the "biological clock" make the change.

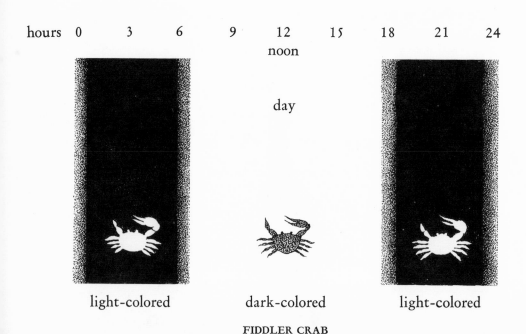

| hours | 0 | 3 | 6 | 9 | 12 noon | 15 | 18 | 21 | 24 |

day

light-colored   dark-colored   light-colored

FIDDLER CRAB

Fiddler crabs also have an activity pattern controlled by the same internal clock. During high tide, they remain inactive in their burrows and are pale in color. At low tide, they emerge, become active, and grow darker. Their deepest color appears fifty minutes later each day, and so does the low tide. But again, if fiddler crabs are kept in a laboratory far away from the sea, they still show changes that follow the rhythm of the tides.

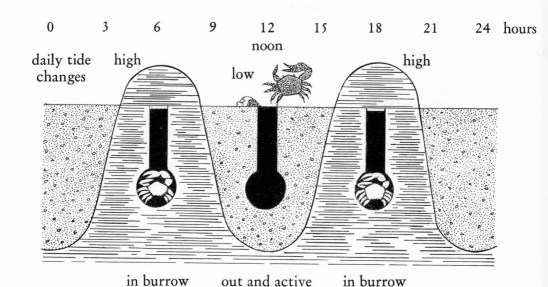

FIDDLER CRAB

Hormones are responsible for the crab's size, growth, and color change. They also control the amount of salt and water in the crab's body. A rapid change from salt to freshwater can kill a crab, yet many crabs move from salt water to fresh and from fresh to salt. The adjustment is made in the crab's gills, which, in response to a hormone signal, let more or less salt pass through.

Crabs that move to and from salt water need time to adjust. This may take from several hours to several days. Most marine crabs can only stand water slightly less salty than the ocean. The coconut, Australian, rock, and mangrove flat crabs adjust well. The wool-handed crab of Europe does so well that it grows and matures in freshwater, and then returns to the sea to spawn.

Crabs of all sizes can be found. The smallest, only 2 millimeters long, lives inside sand dollars, which are relatives of sea urchins. One of the largest is the Japanese spider crab. It grows to 35 centimeters across the shell and 4 meters from one extended leg to the other. The Tasmanian crab reaches a length of 40 centimeters across the shell and weighs up to 15 kilograms.

actual size

SMALLEST CRAB

The largest crab can be as much as 800 times larger than the smallest when both are measured with their legs extended.

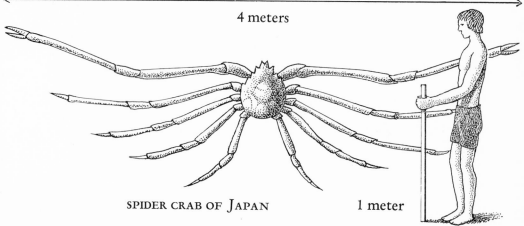

4 meters

SPIDER CRAB OF JAPAN   1 meter

Crabs come in all colors and combinations of colors. Green, blue, and gray are most common. Blue crabs, green crabs, and some others are named for their color. The shape and form of the crab's body vary also. Some are round or oval; some are angular.

Here are ancestors, relatives, and some families of crabs that show the range of this small but varied group of crustaceans.

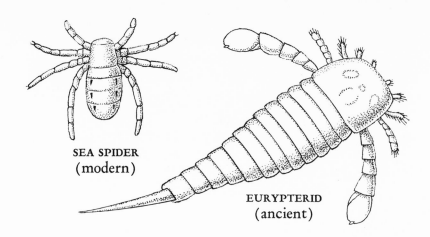

SEA SPIDER
(modern)

EURYPTERID
(ancient)

Crabs are probably the descendants of wormlike marine animals that lived in the seas some 600 million years ago. All crustaceans and related groups came from these segmented creatures, and the changes were under way long before any land animals existed. One early group, now extinct, was the trilobites. The eurypterids, up to three meters long, were not very different from the horseshoe crabs that are still alive today. No remains of true crabs, shrimps, or lobsters have been found in rocks more than 200 million years old. But 200 million years or so was ample time to develop all the kinds of crabs we know today.

PERIPATUS
a living relative of a possible ancestor of crabs

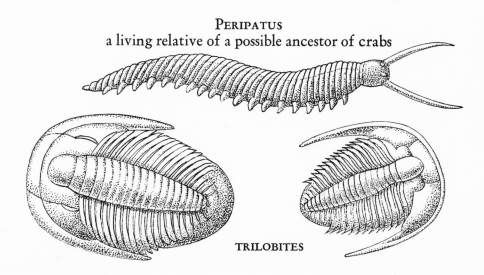

TRILOBITES

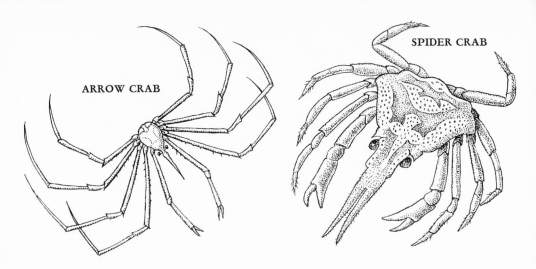

ARROW CRAB

SPIDER CRAB

Spider crabs, of the family Majidae, with long, thin legs, resemble giant spiders. They live in water up to 600 meters deep. All have more or less triangular shells. The largest spider crabs are 4 meters from the tip of the longest leg to the tip of its opposite; the smallest is only 4 centimeters across.

Box, or shamefaced, crabs, of the family Calappidae, get their odd name from their large, flat claws that fit close to their shell, covering and protecting their "face." With these claws they push sand forward to make a shelter. Box crabs are found to depths of 250 meters. The calico crabs, of shallower water, have well-marked patches of bright colors.

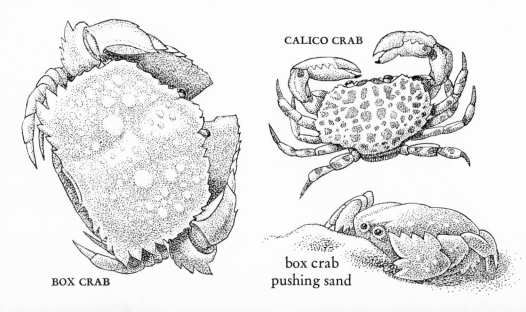

CALICO CRAB

BOX CRAB

box crab
pushing sand

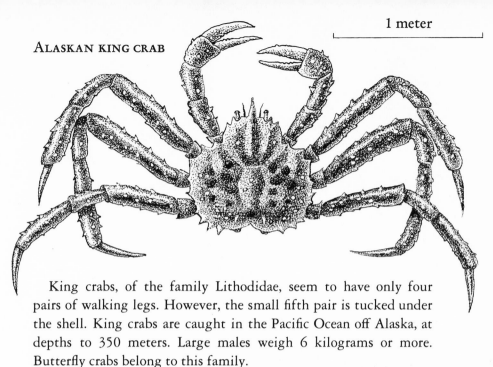

ALASKAN KING CRAB

1 meter

King crabs, of the family Lithodidae, seem to have only four pairs of walking legs. However, the small fifth pair is tucked under the shell. King crabs are caught in the Pacific Ocean off Alaska, at depths to 350 meters. Large males weigh 6 kilograms or more. Butterfly crabs belong to this family.

Ghost crabs, of the family Ocypodidae, are land crabs with square shells, which may help give them better balance. At the center of the shell is an H-shaped depression. Ghost crabs feed at night in the debris washed up by the surf. They are so light-colored they are almost invisible in the sand.

GHOST CRAB

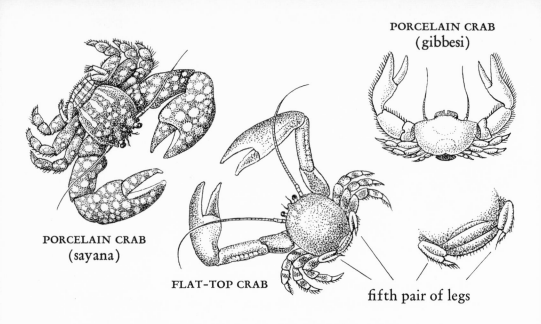

PORCELAIN CRAB
(gibbesi)

PORCELAIN CRAB
(sayana)

FLAT-TOP CRAB

fifth pair of legs

Porcelain crabs, family Porcellanidae, are named for their hard, polished shells. All are small crabs, less than 3 centimeters across. They hide on the bottom of warm or tropical seas, amid coral and broken shells. The fifth pair of legs, small and feeble, is folded in and rests on the shell.

Beetle and mole crabs, family Hippidae, live in the surf zone. They prefer to lie buried in the sand with only the antennae exposed. Their small oval bodies seem adapted to this kind of life.

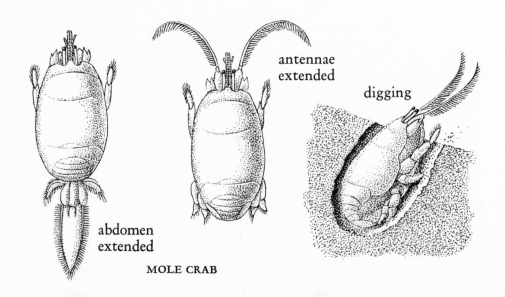

antennae
extended

digging

abdomen
extended

MOLE CRAB

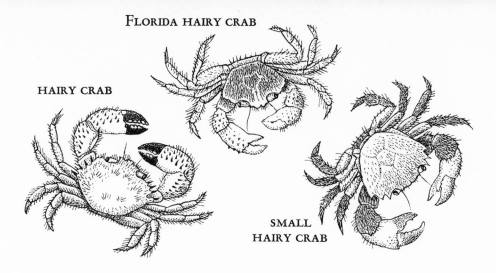

FLORIDA HAIRY CRAB

HAIRY CRAB

SMALL
HAIRY CRAB

Hairy crabs, of the family Xanthidae, are found on both coasts of North America. Hairs cover the upper surface of their legs and their pincers, which have tips colored dark brown, white, or red. Hairy crabs live from the low-tide mark to depths of about 150 meters. Some, as the edible stone crab of the South, are commercially important.

Rock and Jonah crabs, of the family Cancridae, include common shore species of temperate North America and Europe, where several kinds are caught and marketed. Most have oval or six-sided shells. Although related to the swimming crabs, they have no legs adapted for swimming.

ROCK CRAB   JONAH CRAB

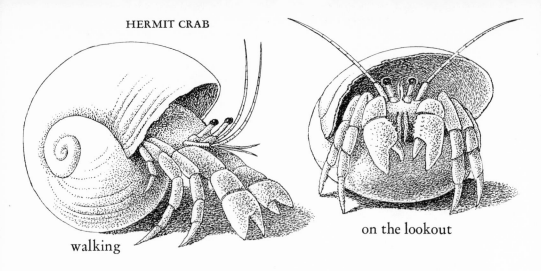

walking

on the lookout

Hermit crabs, family Paguridae, are unusual creatures. Their own shell does not completely protect their body, so they use the cast-off shell of sea snails to cover their soft spiral abdomen. The hermit crab backs into this shell and carries it as a house. If the shell fits well, the hermit crab can retreat into it, blocking the entrance with its large pincers. As hermit crabs grow they discard one shell and try to find a larger one. Hermit crabs live in the sea to depths of nearly 2000 meters, but some species are found on land, quite far from the shore. All seem to be scavengers, feeding on plant material and similar debris. Land hermit crabs make interesting pets. They can be kept in cages and fed with table scraps.

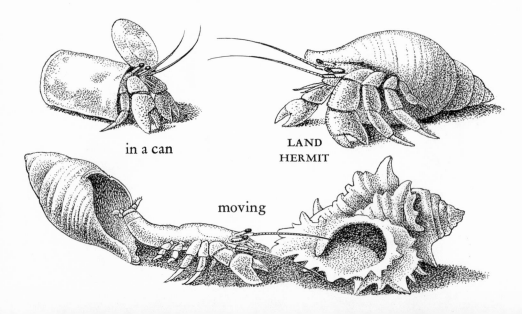

in a can

LAND
HERMIT

moving

The color of crabs often serves to conceal the animal from its enemies. Crabs that live in the floating beds of sargassum seaweed are olive, brown, and yellow, with mottling and spots to match their home. The ghost crab, gray or white, matches the color of the sand dunes on which it lives. Both of these color patterns and others make crabs almost invisible.

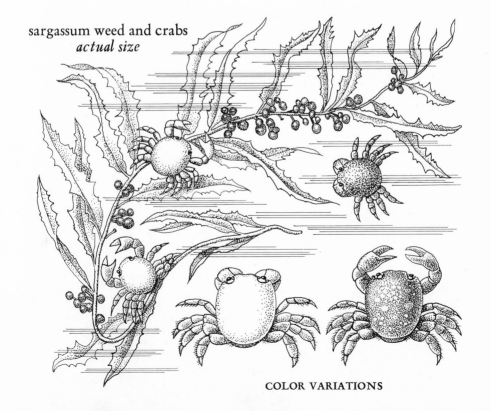

sargassum weed and crabs
actual size

COLOR VARIATIONS

Crabs seek other ways in which to live, feed, hide, and protect themselves. Some crabs seem to decorate or cover their shell with living animals. Sponges, seaweed, and even empty seashells are also used. One brightly colored red crab from Bermuda carries a seashell overhead with two of its legs. The body surface of an Indian Ocean crab is sculptured like a piece of old coral in the reefs where it lives. Many spider crabs attach bits of living sponge and seaweed to their shell. These additions grow and make the crab's shell blend with other life on the bottom.

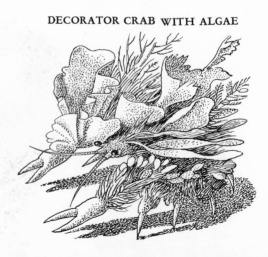

DECORATOR CRAB WITH ALGAE

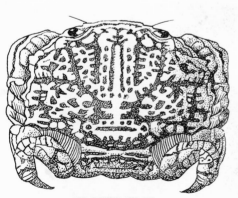

ERODED CRAB

Marine hermit crabs live in shells to which they sometimes attach living sponges and sea anemones. The coral-gall crab irritates the growing tips of coral so that the coral grows up around the female crab, entrapping her in a stony coral house. She lives there all her protected life, laying her eggs and guarding her broods of young.

Other crabs live inside living animals or within their shells. They all belong to the same family and are called pea crabs because of their small size, 1 to 15 millimeters. The soft-bodied females live inside oysters, mussels, clams, and even in sea cucumbers.

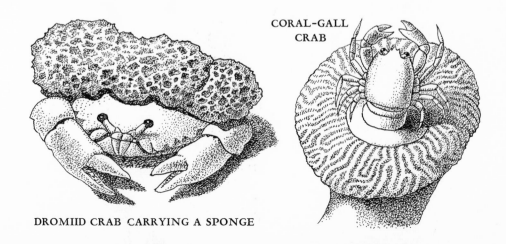

CORAL-GALL CRAB

DROMIID CRAB CARRYING A SPONGE

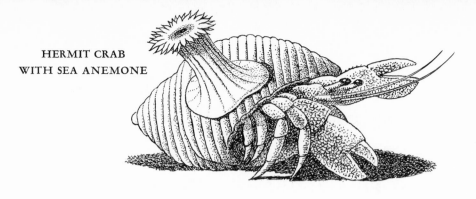

These odd partnerships between crabs
and other sea life may benefit both. Neither
seems to take anything of importance from
the other, but one or both may have a better
chance to survive with this arrangement.
Crabs often select a specific plant or animal
for the partnership. The hermit crab chooses
a particular kind of sponge or sea anemone
to attach to its shell.

Crabs, when not active, hide under or
between rocks, coral, or amid seaweeds or
other sea plants. Some burrow in sand, mud,
and even into soft rock. Land crabs make
burrows too, sometimes damaging gardens.

The depth of a crab burrow depends upon the amount of moist sand or soil available. Mole crabs, when washed out of the sand by the surf, quickly dig backward into the soft sand until only their antennae stick out. The dune-inhabiting ghost crab may have to dig to a depth of one meter to reach moist sand, as his burrow is sometimes 300 meters from the ocean. Moisture is essential, both to hold the sand firm in the burrow and to keep the crab's gills damp.

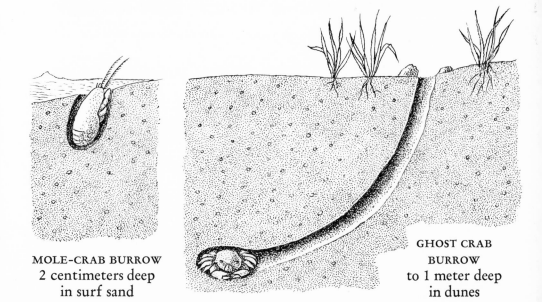

MOLE-CRAB BURROW
2 centimeters deep
in surf sand

GHOST CRAB
BURROW
to 1 meter deep
in dunes

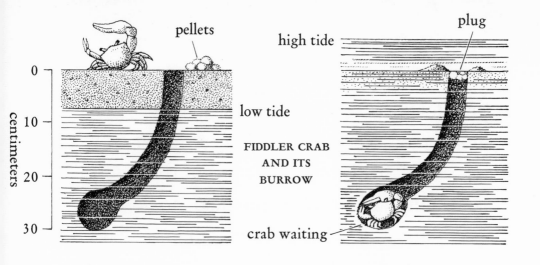

pellets

high tide

plug

low tide

FIDDLER CRAB
AND ITS
BURROW

crab waiting

The fiddler crabs live on sand beaches and in mud marshes between the high- and low-tide marks. They dig their burrows 30 centimeters or so deep and carry the sand or mud to the surface in small pellets. At the entrance of the burrow pellets are put in piles or are pushed away. When the tide comes in, the fiddler returns to its shelter. It plugs the entrance with wet sand or mud and waits till the next low tide before coming out again to feed.

Crabs are eaten by many of the backboned animals that live in the sea or along the shore. Bottom-feeding fish like the drum, angelfish, puffer, grouper, and sea bass feed on small crabs. Some of these fish have special ridged teeth for grinding the shells of crabs and shellfish. Shorebirds like gulls, dowitchers, curlews, and snipes turn over stones or probe into the mud for small crabs also. The crab-eating plover of East Africa and Asia is so named for the food it eats. These shorebirds feed on crabs and mollusks, which they open with their heavy bills.

CRAB PLOVER

CRAB-EATING MACAQUE

Alligators, crocodiles, and some tur-tles eat crabs also. So do a few mammals. Sea otters hunt them regularly. Raccoons go down to the shore for food, and crabs are a part of their diet. They are also the food of a Southeast Asian monkey, the crab-eating macaque. This monkey lives along the shores and in mangrove swamps. There small crabs are usually plentiful, but fruits and grains may be limited. Other kinds of macaques sometimes feed the same way.

Only a few kinds of crabs are used as food by man. We want the large kinds with enough meat to make them worth catching. The kinds we eat must be numerous enough to supply the marketplace, so people who can afford crabs can get them when they want them. Large land crabs are caught for food on some Caribbean islands where they are considered a delicacy.

TWO WAYS OF CATCHING CRABS

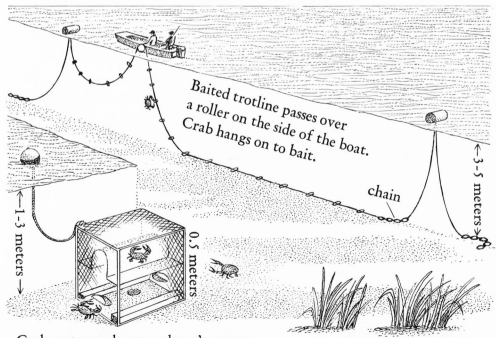

Baited trotline passes over a roller on the side of the boat. Crab hangs on to bait.

chain

←3-5 meters→

←1-3 meters→

0.5 meters

Crabs enter crab pot and can't escape.

Most crabs that people eat are taken from shallow water. They are caught in nets, traps, and "pots." Best known of the edible crabs is the blue crab of the Atlantic, which sometimes moves up rivers into freshwater. Next is the king crab of the north Pacific. These two kinds account for more than three quarters of the total crab catch of almost a million pounds a year. Also taken for food are a dozen other kinds of crabs, including the stone, Jonah, green, deep-sea red, Samoan, Dungeness, tanner, and Kona.

EDIBLE CRABS

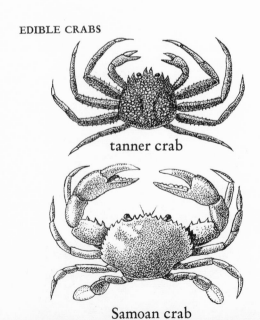

tanner crab

Samoan crab

Fish and some other animals eat crabs whole. They choose the smaller kinds.
We want the delicious meat that is mainly in the crab's legs, so we select

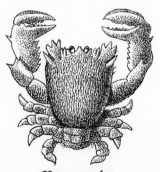

Kona crab

The meat of the crab is actually the muscles in or connected to the legs or pincers, which are the preferred parts for eating.

Edible crabs are marketed in several ways. Live crabs and fresh crab meat are usually available only near the place where the crabs are caught. Both hard-shelled and soft-shelled blue crabs are sold alive. Sometimes whole cooked crabs appear in the market. More often parts of the crab, especially the claws, are sold. Stone crabs are marketed in this way.

the larger ones. People eat over a dozen kinds of crabs, such as the blue crab. Some of the others most commonly seen in markets are shown on these pages.

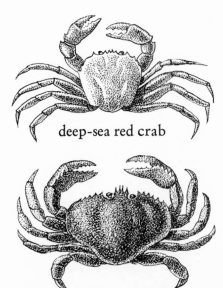

deep-sea red crab

stone crab

Dungeness crab

Crabs are also cooked and broken open. The meat is picked out and sold fresh. The claws of stone and king crabs are cooked or sent frozen to market, so they can be prepared quickly in restaurants.

When crabs are to be sold at a distance, they are prepared for market by freezing or canning. Today people almost anyplace in the world can have crabs to eat. Most canned crab meat comes from Japan and other Far Eastern countries, where fishing is more common and where more labor is available for the hard work of picking out the meat and processing it. Recently machines have been invented to break crabs open and take out the meat.

Crabs have been on earth for much longer than man. These curious creatures play a small but interesting natural role in the environment. Our large harvests of edible crabs have reduced their number. But more important, the pollution of bays, harbors, and beaches together with the drainage and destruction of seaside swamps may wipe out some crab populations entirely. Because we are all a part of nature, what we do to help crabs survive is likely to help human beings survive also.

BASHFUL CRAB

INDEX

indicates illustration